T0042929

A knife so sharp its edge cannot be seen

A knife
so sharp
its edge
cannot
be seen

Erin Noteboom

Brick Books

Library and Archives Canada Cataloguing in Publication

Title: A knife so sharp its edge cannot be seen / Erin Noteboom.
Names: Noteboom, Erin, 1972- author.
Description: Poems.
Identifiers: Canadiana (print) 20220489300 | Canadiana (ebook) 20220489335 |
ISBN 9781771316026 (softcover) | ISBN 9781771316033 (EPUB) |
ISBN 9781771316040 (PDF)
Classification: LCC PS8577.O7525 K65 2023 | DDC C811/.6—dc23

We gratefully acknowledge the Canada Council for the Arts, the Government of Canada
through the Canada Book Fund, and the Ontario Arts Council for their support of our
publishing program.

Edited by Nick Thran.
Cover image: Science Photo Library.
Author photo by Wayfinder Bow.
The book is set in Miller.
Design by Marijke Friesen.
Printed and bound by Coach House Printing.

Brick Books
487 King St. W.
Kingston, ON
K7L 2X7
www.brickbooks.ca

Though much of the work of Brick Books takes place on the ancestral lands of the
Anishinaabeg, Haudenosaunee, Huron-Wendat, and Mississaugas of the Credit
peoples, our editors, authors, and readers from many backgrounds are situated from
coast to coast to coast in Canada on the traditional and unceded territories of over six
hundred nations who have cared for Turtle Island from time immemorial. While living
and working on these lands, we are committed to hearing and returning the rightful
imaginative space to the poetries, songs, and stories that have been untold, under-told,
wrongly told, and suppressed through colonization.

Contents

We could begin with the crab that scratches in the sand

You could begin with the crab that scratches in the sand. The name of the animal is the action or sound it makes, or its color. The name parents other like meanings belonging to other things, leaving the animal behind: grapho (Greek—to scratch, and so, to write), gramma (the scratches), graph, grammar, grab.
—Susan Brind Morrow, *The Names of Things*

We could begin with the cut—in sticks, in bone,
in clay, in stone, we learn to hold
a thought pinched like a cowrie shell.
We drill and thread it on the breath
like the song of a bird. And call it word.

We could begin with the hole—the one
in the needle. Fifty centuries older than the wheel
and made at first from the bones of birds.
Needles in our hands and we were walking.
In cold we could live inside the ones
we killed.

Linguists say the oldest words are *hand*
and *give* and *ash* and *burn*. Hand me the ash
and let us mark the world.
The caves in which we leave our pictures
are chosen in part to hold our singing.
We know a sacred place by how it listens,
answers. These hollow places hold our breath

like beads. Take our bones and leave us
meaning.

Let us take the honey from the hive
until all that's left is sting and sweetness.
Let us write in wax and heat our scratches.
Encaustic, caustic, ink. It means
to burn. And soon to boil
feathers—that smell—or better still
to soak and plunge in heated sand.
A quick hook with knife and we have made a pen.
Let us take a skin—stretched and stripped
and cured. Thinnest along the spine where—
again—we fold.

Let us turn like wheels in water,
let us thunder, hammer, pulp,
and re-learn paper. Let us turn
to type, which means to punch.
Let us melt and pour the shimmering metal:
Foundry, found, font—lost.
Let us take the Doves Type
and print Milton, words of grab
and gasp and tumble.
Let us bundle up the punches:
twelve hundred pounds of lead
wrapped in grudge and canvas,
and given to the river. Lost.

Recovered. And we begin
with a font designer larking the mud flats.

Among the coins and combs, the pipes
and pottery, the thickened keys and lamps for Diwali
a hundred characters flicker crabwise,
here and there, back into the world.

Some terms used in texts

Memory

They say heart of Jeanne d'Arc could not be burned
in the fire that killed her.
Imagine instead it could not be quenched.
See it lifted from the ash and held aloft,
ablaze and speaking.

Metaphor

Deep in our history
a bowl of milk
became the moon.

Perspective

Parting, my father holds me
like a newspaper.
Says, "I can't get far enough away
to see you."

Specifics

The graveyard at dawn.
The stonecutter
parks a red pickup,
slowly blasts a name.

Recombination

One day, the universe
became transparent.
This has nothing to do with love.

Structure

When a strange frost killed his beloved orchids,
English eccentric Edward James built a garden
of concrete, upright and immune
to ice. In time,
the vines entangled it.

Niche

There is for each hollow of the world
a thing that is held. November was empty
until the chrysanthemums bloomed.

History

After the war, Mathew Brady
went bankrupt, glass negatives sold to creditors.
Useless for windows, of course, but greenhouses—
The dead of Antietam lose their shadows
across the drifts of ferns
and orchids.

Storytelling

In Nagasaki, after, only the smokestacks
were left standing. They were spared
by vortex shedding—round sides sloughing wind.
Nothing to do with symbol,
though the urge towards symbol
is irresistible. This freighted world.
Oh help us carry it.

skiagraphs

Ghost Ring

*In 1895, Wilhelm Röntgen was experimenting with cathode tubes in
a darkened lab when he noticed a glow coming from the other side of
the laboratory—something was striking the phosphorescent screen he
had stashed there. He experimented for months to better understand
these X-rays—"X" for unknown—and discovered they could show
him the shadow of his bones. He used the rays to expose photographic
plates, including an image of his wife Bertha's hand and their wedding
ring. Radiation folklore has it that on seeing the image, Frau Röntgen
exclaimed: "I have seen my death."*

It's not that I know nothing.

I know a candle set behind a globe of water
is enough to do the stitching

when winter light fails. There is always needlework.
Even the wives of gentlemen scientists

are slowly squinting blind.
I understand focus. How the yellow glow

on the whipstitch of the white sheet
thickens the shadows in floors and corners.

I know light changes us.
Wilhelm set a plate and led me

to the laboratory in holy astonishment.
A quarter hour with my hand still,

the clock chime, a gasp. In the unveiled negative,
my flesh is half-life,

my bones less solid than the ghost
of our ring. For history he records

my cry. And lets it seem ignorance.
As if I didn't know

light pierces us. The first diagnostic X-ray
will be of a needle, embedded

in a woman's hand.

Skiagraphs, 1896

When the smoke from dry wood comes between the eye of the observer and
some dark space it appears blue. So the atmosphere appears blue because
of the darkness which is beyond it ...
—Leonardo da Vinci

Hobnails in boots and buckshot in shoulders,
the openings between an infant's bones.
The surface like the century
falls away, the skin pinned and lifted,
the flesh turned to fogs and backgrounds.
There is a colour that means distance.
In Da Vinci's paintings, for instance,
far off hills or towers are awash in scattered photons.
As with a charcoal curve softened
by the pad of the thumb, our lungs become
that blue and intricate. At first this class of image
has no one name: radiogram, fluoroscope,
X-ray. Skiagraph—meaning to scratch
with shadows. Soon a hundred thousand children
will look down to see their shoes made vitreous,
their toes ajoint and wiggling.

Curie Abundant

Like raspberries in their fever, like blueberries at the end of July,
uranium ore is heaped in a Paris courtyard—
mine tailings dark and welted,
black and bruised. They shovel it into bushels,
scrape-drag them into the shed, pick out the pine needles.
The whole day mixing the boiling mass
with an iron rod nearly as large as myself.
Extract and separate. Wash and fraction.
It is such heavy and such female work.
Four years of labour. Four hundred tons of heating coal.

Pierre and Marie work together. Their lab, *a miserable old shed*
formerly used for the dissection of cadavers.
The slag pile outside, adrift with needles,
falls. A frost, a snow, a thaw, a spring.
A frost, a snow, a thaw, a spring,
and the dust is rising. Their hands entwine
in notes, in volumes. Such heavy
and such female work—and charge
is rising. Coal dust, they call it. Iron dust.
It's that. It's more. The air conducts.
Their clothes crackle as if on the winter line.

I cannot express the untroubled quietness
of those seasons. The shed is summer kitchen, winter kitchen.
The roof is glass. The floor is bitumen.
It is miserable in all seasons.
The separation is largely by washing—

radium, less soluble, falling first
out of the vats of solution.
Forty tons of corrosive chemicals.
Four hundred tons of water. And pinprick by pinprick,
radium chloride—point one of a gram at last aglow
like jam on a windowsill.

Curie in Love

*If a radioactive substance is placed in the dark in the vicinity of the closed
eye or of the temple, a sensation of light fills the eye.*
—Marie Curie, doctoral dissertation, 1903

The sensation of light
is light. There is no way for her to know it.
She is so young and so in love, marrying
an equal, choosing for her gown a navy dress
she can wear in laboratories. Hand in hand
they slip through the university courtyard—
Pierre and Marie Curie, in the world before the war.
*One of our joys was to go into our workroom at night
to perceive on all sides the feebly luminous silhouettes—
the bottles and capsules of our work.* That light
marbles and embarnacles them both,
turns their fingers strange and fibrous.
Soon enough he cannot rise from bed.
It was really a lovely sight and always new to us.
She loses twenty pounds. Two pregnancies.
There is no way for her to know
that her light will soon paint gunsights
and watch dials. That it is ticking through her body,
his body, faster than time. What she has understood
is astonishing enough: the atom, active.
It is as if marbles were found to be breathing out.
As if stones were found to speak.
Sick and stumbling, Pierre is struck
by a cart of military equipage. He passes untouched

under the hooves of six horses. Untouched
between the front wheels, between the turns
of chance and miracle, before six tons
and the back wheel open his skull
and kill him instantly.
The coffin slaps closed.
And the deterministic world.

That light.

She has no way of knowing
it is ionizing radiation, lighting the eye gel
the way a cooling pool is lit
around a great reactor. Her hair was thick then,
and thickly piled. Her fingers smooth.
Her thighs like marble. She closes her eyes
and raises the vial.

Curie in Grief

Short as a half-drawn breath
this life. I have no desire to die.
I have, in fact, no desire.
Radium's half-life: sixteen hundred years.
Sixteen hundred cars and carts:
on the curb I stand and count.
Fingers close around my finger.
My rings and bracelets: oh my daughters.
One is six and one just walking.
My heir and my biographer.
My half-orphans. Count their fingers round
my wrists and fingers.

Radium Girls

I would be only too happy to give any aid that I could. However, there is absolutely no means of destroying the substance once it enters the human body.
—Marie Curie in 1927, commenting to the press on the lawsuit by the "Radium Girls": five women, each dying of radiation poisoning, formerly employed by the US Radium Corporation to paint clock faces

Her boot heels hooked on the rung of her tall stool,
Amelia Maggia, a dial painter, a radium girl,
pausing to lick the brush to a fine point
between the dots at six and seven.

Their boot heels hooked on the rungs of tall stools,
The dial painters, the radium girls,
their hair chignoned, their shirtwaists buttoned.
A paint called Undark on the hands and numbers—

gunsights in the war and, later, clocks.
Four factories across fourteen years. Four thousand girls.
On breaks they paint their nails and buttons,
surprise their husbands with their Alice smiles—

then vanish. One by one, their teeth come loose.
Their hair and youth fall into undark pain.
Amelia Maggia loses her jaw. They call it syphilis.
She's buried quietly.

They call it syphilis—she's buried quietly.
She has two sisters, Albina and Quinta,
their boot heels hooked on tall stools.
A rolling kiss to point the brush

six times a dial. Piecework-paid, they paint
two hundred a day. Close cousin to calcium, the radium
buttons into bones. In the dark
their lips glow faintly. The sisters, laughing.

Albina's wedding dress has three dozen buttons.
Her husband laughs and fumbles; they glow faintly.
The tick of their heels as they dance in the century.
And one by one those girls are shut in

urns and boxes. The undark pain.
Their hair in clumps. Their shirtwaists buttoned.
The dial painters, the radium girls. The four thousand.
Impossible to say what happened

to all of them. But these were sisters.
Quinta's hips both break. Albina loses all her teeth
and children. And Amelia Maggia, five years dead,
is lifted from her grave. Her skull made powder.

Her long bones sliced to two-inch buttons.
She's scraps now. She's spatter. But her dazzling bones
can still expose an X-ray film. That fog and stars,
her sisters' map. Their fate. Their evidence.

Curie in Notebooks

Solvay, 1911

Those quantum boys
with their talk of uncertainty
and observation. They don't understand
how a woman can walk through walls.

America, 1920

Niagara Falls. The Brooklyn Zoo.
Celebrities and lobster dinners.
When they talk about my splendid work
it seems to me I'm already dead—
that I am looking at myself dead.
The First Lady gives her white roses.
She presses them between the heavy pages
of her work.

Last notebook, 1934

Sixty-six. It's amazing
that she's lived this long.
Her fingers wrapped in ropey scars.
Her eyes four times cut open.
In laboratory margins she records
her temperature,
her weight and dis-
charges—

The heart can heal and here is how we know

There is a pulse in every piece of us
that tells how close we come
to bomb tests. To Trinity, to Upshot–Knothole

and Castle-Bravo. To the flashed men at Buster–Jangle,
the struck ships at Bikini Atoll. These clouds rose up
like pillars of salt. And the body looks backward.

Across eighteen years these clouds rise like pillars
of salt, and the body looks backward.
In each cell our DNA is knit in carbon loops and tattings.
The slipped stitch of isotope tacks its ticking label
in every part of us. Thus

we know that bones, to our surprise, are quicker
than skin, that long hair reaches backward
like a pen. That things we once thought fixed

can change. The neurons of learning.
The strange glass of the eye.
The heart, as we might have guessed,

heals patchwork, beating cells here old, here new,
while outside the snow is falling into April,
freckling the cracked black wood

of the century apple, fresh with bloom.

What is Eden but a thing that's lost

Silently, a wolf enters the schoolhouse.
Slipping over the sill, she pads the classroom,
snuffles through the grove of upturned chairs.
Mushrooms in the building blocks, bright books flapping open,
a microscope gone blind. Outside the yellow Ferris wheel
squeaks and sways but does not turn. The bears enter,
the mink and boar, the ancient horses.
Blackberry brambles choke the residential blocks.
Poplars crack the hospital. This is Chernobyl,
and what haunts it is both vast
and subtle. You could name it time:
the twentieth century growing points like a stag,
belling, branching like daughter particles,
thickening like rust, which is just
slow fire. Cut down the apple
and throw out your spinning wheels.
Your failsafes will not save you. In its tower
the city clock grows muddy with the nests
of swallows, its ticks—until it stops—
so faint and tender. Out where roses tangle
through the wild, a spider spins a web off-centre.

beauty/cost

A knife so sharp its edge cannot be seen—

A knife so sharp its edge cannot be seen—
early hands knapped these in flint, obsidian,
and some survived, too fine to use
on anything but shadows. Too soon for art,
but we struggle for another label.
Experiment, perhaps, or craft attenuated.
I think we built a world
of useless beauty—
a knowledge sharper than the blade.
The sky flash of a blue jay. The pollen
in the grave.

Given paint, a starving man

Given paint, a starving man
will paint. Given bones to burn
we burn them and again
make paint. Those reindeer
in the deep cool caves are made
from reindeer bones. Those horses
from the blood of horses. Ancient hands
are made from breath, and longing
is bottomless. There are moths
that are born with no mouths.
They are not intended to live
beyond the tangling of genes,
the egg-laying. They are moths
and so do not, presumably, feel love.
But hunger? Imagine them.
Do you not feel hunger?

Imprisoned, al Haytham makes notes on the nature of light

Abū Ali al-Hasan ibn al-Haytham, a tenth-century philosopher and physicist, wrote his great Book of Optics *during his ten years as a political prisoner.*

I think it cannot be as the ancients say,
that the eye is lighthouse, and sweeps its beam
across the walls and rags.
For if light has its source inside the eye, then why
does light after darkness—the sun, say,
when I am given window—why does that sting?
Surely that is something entering, like a needle
or a sword. It is true, yes, that we see
that on which our gaze alights, and yet,
when gaze is shuttered,
does not the thing unlooked on still shine?
I remember perfect apricots,
favoured by the radiance of God. I must believe
they are still favoured, though I cannot see them.
Today they remembered my lentils
in a bowl of plain scratched tin. I ate
and licked, then set the empty thing
into a slice of sun. And behold,
a ray struck the bowl, and from it, bounced.
Exactly like a marble. I knelt down to see,
knelt down as if to play at marbles,

and the dust on my hands seemed innocent.
I cupped them in prayer and felt
the warm regard of light upon them.
In the beam, motes swirled around me
like writing. I think no eye does this.
No human eye.

The sadness of engineers

          is knowledge.
Mister Thomas Andrews, ship designer,
descends the grand staircase.
Behind him, the clock: Honour and Glory
crowning time. It's after midnight. *Titanic* is sinking.
In the first-class smoking parlour,
Mister Thomas Andrews lingers at the fire.
He knows the numbers: Lifeboats
and passengers. The capacity of pumps.
The rate of loss of heat in water.
His hands twitch as if to roll out blueprints.
Off the listing mantle,
candles slide.

Pavlovsk Station

Outside Leningrad, the scientists
are digging up potatoes. It is 1941. The Germans closing in.
The scientists, men and women, are from the seed vault
at Pavlovsk Station. Their work is to save
the six thousand kinds of potatoes,
the two hundred varieties of edible cherry.
It will not be easy. There are rats,
and men even hungrier.
There is bread made of sawdust.
Jam made of wallpaper. For 872 days,
Leningrad folds inward like a fertilized flower.
640,000 dead, and mostly of starvation—but these
are merely numbers. In the heart, at the bottom,
in the basement of Pavlovsk Station, the scientists
starve with seeds in their pockets.
The one in charge of rice lies cradled
in the sacks of rice.

The Common Swift

Consider in its turn the common swift.
There is new evidence that a swift can stay aloft
two hundred days. Scientists are puzzled,
not over how, but why. Consider the work, they note,
of sleeping in flight: the alertness demanded,
the tacks and turns it takes
to lean on wind. Even a gliding bird would expend
a small but constant effort.
For such a cost, there must be benefit.
That is the equation of science, which is only
half a turn from love. Consider a marriage,
surely no less common, or marvellous,
than swifts. Surely no less a nest
built on the air.

The Bus Stop

Outside the Benrath Senior Care Centre in Dusseldorf,
the caretakers have placed a bus stop.
A bench and a shelter. A graceful tree.
The bus does not come there. But those who wander
stop and wait. The private with marching orders,
the baker who must awaken dough. The woman who knows
she is fourteen years old. She must get home.
Her mother will worry. Every day, she waits.
Most days, a nurse comes to wait with her,
brings water in the heat, or mittens in that season.
Because the woman believes she is going home,
she is not frightened. Or at least, she is patient and brave.
She sits with her hands folded inside the mittens
and waits like Mary for the birth of the Word.
The bus is not coming, and soon enough
she will forget why she is waiting
and be coaxed inside for soup. But for now
the sun gleams through the roof of the shelter,
and lays its hand against the side of her face. A lie, yes,
but the sweetest lie God ever told us: Of course
I am coming. Of course you can go home.

light/cage

Every year on September 11th, eighty-eight searchlights
line the foundations of the fallen towers,
and push their hollow shapes as tall
as light can reach. *Hollow*
because the searchlights also make a cage
that captures birds. Thousands, sometimes, baffled
by the beams they take for solid. Migrating,
they are drawn as if to a smacking window,
as if to the moon on water, and once inside our loss
they exhaust themselves in turning, in making the beams
flash with wings as white as moth or mirror. We know this.
We know it before we turn them on, these towers made of gauze.
And we know them, the birds who are lost. They are the cost
of the beauty. The beauty of the cost.

ghazals

Ghazal beginning with a couplet by Lorna Crozier

If loss had a language it would be water's.
We are mostly made of it.

Broken string, the pearls scatter.
Shake like teeth from the bathroom rug.

"A soft fight." In English, it means
he didn't hit her.

Cast bones, cast bones—three crows
in an oak tree. Such news.

The sea is comfortless. Say what you want,
it won't cease its sighing, its saying of names.

Landlocked. November trees
say *ocean, ocean, ocean.*

Ghazal beginning with a poem title by Fernec Juhász

A boy changed into a stag cries out
at the gate of secrets.

Put a knife under the bed
to ease a birth.

The first thing you lay in a fire—
a bed of stones.

Woodpecker in the chimney. Mouse bones
in the bottom of a jar.

Look for owls in daylight.
Count and charm the crows.

And be patient. One hundred times each second,
lightning strikes.

Ghazal beginning with lines by Yiannis Ritsos

I know that each one of us travels to love alone,
alone to faith and to death.

When preparing to lower yourself into a well,
first send down a candle. It breathes like you.

I dream about the war. Almost every night.
Or sometimes that I have misplaced my child.

Learn to walk as if you had a different history.
Toes unpointed. A hand that never knew a knife.

There is a wildness in God's mercy.
I misread the hymnal. Think of hawks.

I am preoccupied with angels.
Their pulse and fur. Their eyes and openings.

Ghazal beginning with lines by János Pilinszky

Birds, the sun, and again birds.
By night, what will be left of me?

Don't you think the lily speaks to the bee?
Or the bee to the sun, dancing obeisance.

Certain songs are older than language.
We could drum before we could talk.

By ten to one, the ants outweigh us.
But what of sorrow?

Of all things in the living world, only snow
does not love us.

We are each going to a white and windowless house
across a crust that barely holds.

Ghazal beginning with lines by Theodore Roethke

The river turns on itself,
The tree retreats into its own shadow.

Like a breath, the bay empties
before the wave.

Old photographs. Setting fire to them—
almost a murder.

. . . as sparks fly upward, the Bible says.
But they do, as if reaching.

A cicada year. Even now they are sleeping
under the earth.

Ghazal beginning with lines by Wisława Szymborska

When I pronounce the word Future,
the first syllable already belongs to the past.

Twisting in the wind—I don't mean laundry.
There's a shadow in the language, a long stain on the city walls.

Tailing ancestors through graveyards. Husband or father,
it's a man's name we're buried under.

I dream a hallway, dark with all doors shut.
Behind one, a shadow shifts its weight.

I hardly know what to do next.
Do I breathe in or out?

Two rivers in one valley.
Let's call them Prosper, Sorrow.

Ghazal beginning with lines by Anna Akhmatova

You will hear thunder and remember me,
And think: she wanted storms.

Volcanic sunrise. The day falls open
like a dead rose.

Living crèche: the redhead dressed as Mary
shivers.

The wreck of a tree is larger than a tree.
When my father fell I could not catch him.

How long can a house stand empty?
A bare elm hanging from the hook of the moon.

Ghazal beginning with lines by Pablo Neruda

So close that your hand on my chest is my hand,
so close that your eyes close as I fall asleep.

Mary, I wonder: did the baby Christ sleep
with his arms flung open?

As the sun never sees a shadow,
so the dead don't grieve.

The heart like an atom
is brightest in its splits.

Child's Bible. My daughter confuses
ghosts and angels.

Sometimes it seems like a cold road home.

*poems with movement toward
the particular*

Untitled poem with one shoe in it

On the green transformer box by the bus stop, someone has set
an infant's shoe. Lost, and put there so it might be seen.
It is the leather slipper kind,
white with an appliqué of cherries. And this
is memory: lifted, lighted, singular.
Then I turn the corner
and the whole street is thick
with Japanese lilac, freshly bloomed
as they were the day my sister died.
This is that day. I had forgotten
the reason for the greyness of my body
though my body nonetheless went grey.
And the truth about the shoe is:
there is no guessing what will be struck
in memory. Think of the chance even in archeology.
Here, the ditch-digger turns up bottles.
Over there, a nest of bones.

Untitled poem about sensitization

As with bee stings, so with grief.
Sometimes something terrible happens.
Sometimes you step on a hive.
Stung three hundred times, you survive.
But always after, the smallest thing
can slay you. Always after,
the smallest thing.

Sorrow first, and then the Fall

Sometimes as large dogs and sometimes as hailstones
the uncontrolled comes into the garden.
No need in this theology for snakes—
we're all making our way bellywise,
just barely holding on. Before she drowned, my sister
traded heat for paintbrushes, spent whole loaves
to gather gulls.

Sometimes as birth and sometimes as blood clots
the magnificent visits. *I magnify*, said Mary,
caught in the teeth of grace. She had to be shaking.
My soul is a ruin with one wind-swept bird
dipping its brilliant head. Save by drifts of sand,
a perfect wall. Dunes shift, my heart uncovering. God the wind.

Sometimes as lightning and sometimes as crickets
the ruins speak. The sound in conch shell
is not the ocean but the echo of blood, a heartbeat magnified
in the folds of silence. Before she drowned my sister shouted,
"Stop the car, stop the car," and took off running
into crows.

The things the dead have touched

What should we do with their socks,
for instance. There is no answer.
We ask, but fingerprints
evaporate. The voice demagnetizes
on the answer tape, the smell of skin
lifts free of sweaters.
From under the driver's seat
I pull a map scrawled on a napkin.
Her lost hand has drawn an asterisk
to mark the Target parking lot.
Not knowing it will be the pole star.
How the whole sky spins.

Letter beginning with news of the weather

I am human and I am here in this place
where you are not. I have been cold,
or hot. The crops have suffered.
There is news about your brother's heart.
There is news about my heart
which is that this pen turns it
like the blade of a plough.
I want to be closer
but know the cut between us
cannot be crossed in words.
I make this thought tidy enough to envelop.
On the drive to town, the yard light
dips below the curve of the world
like a sail.

I keep a box of keys

It is the key that is lost, not the lock,
and yet I keep a box of keys, like a faith
in a God I can no longer name. In the formal portrait
of my great-grandmother's family,
text scratched in the tarnished folds of skirts
names three infants who did not survive: Helen.
Helen. Helen.

Untitled poem with movement toward the particular

A love song, now, for those who tend the wounds,
who manage drainage tubes,
and ragged seepage. For you I sing:
all love is conditional. It depends on recognition.
And, God, that's hard. How sick buries us—
its ranks of pills, its stupid rituals.
It slicks our skin and twists our smell,
and we are mammals, after all—
we sniff towards each other.
I sing, my darling: Many people,
and with less reason, have awakened
after twenty years to find themselves asleep
with strangers. But you once found me
fallen out of the world, adrift in urine
on the kitchen floor. All I remember
is the dark fringe of your eyelashes,
and "Hey"—your husky whisper—
"there you are."

Thank you, thank you very much

It's like that famous moment when Elvis
takes off his Sasquatch Suit, and the universe is revealed
as an irreducible joke. After cancer,
specialists will spend five years telling you
you haven't survived, yet.
Ask them what they'd call this July afternoon
after a blood screening, the bright sky celled with clouds
pressed flat between the slides of temperature,
as you, under the cherry tree lie poised
between the pull of earth
and press of thick grass. The goldfinch strokes twice
in the clear air, dives, curves up again,
and glides the wave of balance
between weight and wings. This moment
has the curves and scallops
of survival, the greens and golds of it.
Remind the specialists of Elvis. His jumpsuit's
damp and rumpled, but rhinestones still
catch light and throw across the world
those little rings of wonder.

too strong to stop,
too sweet to lose

Too strong to stop, too sweet to lose

What was any art but an effort to make a sheath, a mould in which to imprison for a moment the shining, elusive element which is life itself—life hurrying past us and running away, too strong to stop, too sweet to lose?
—Willa Cather

What marks us?

Small things. Blue bead,
missed chance, the rivelled trails
of ants. Consider the marks
of history: the hemlock,
the nails, the moon's face
nocked in sticks. None of these
is great. And smaller than any,
each weathering touch
of rain.

What is our ancient knowledge?

To track by broken grass,
trace the future
in the moon's fogged mirror.
To cast runes from the hand—
that bowl of bone and leather.
Their fall, their scritch and jumble.
The hawk's shift
across a branch of shadow.

What things are lost?

Many. Most. Those that make it,
spared by chance.
Consider the rune poem,
only copy of a pagan text,
bound between Lucy the Martyr
and the date of Easter.
What brought it there?
Or saved that book
from the burning library?

What things are wise?

Mirrors. Keys.
The sow that swallows
the runt of her litter. The bees
that sleep in smoke.
The beekeeper's widow bending her whisper
to the buzzing mouth of the hive.

What things bid us enter?

Windows. Scissors.
The open throats of orchids.
The polished backs of flies.
The heart of the Virgin,
gaudy with swords.
The avalanche that opens
like a ripping page.

What things protect us?

Bread and salt.
Sharpened silver.
Sprigs of mistletoe carried in secret.
Fish-eyed lenses set in heavy doors.
Rhymes and dental records.
Forgetfulness. Distance.

What is the source of power?

Time. Only listen:
the wind in green wheat
makes the sound of a scythe
being sharpened.

What lasts?

Oh, the wrack of history.
The fragment of Sappho
in the mummy of a crocodile.
The dog's grave unearthed
by the Athens Metro—
jaw arranged
on jumbled paw bones.

Why are we restless?

Stir the soup with a knife.
Pull the bread from the oven
singing. Despite our aprons we are angel-natured,
our shoulders ache with wonder.
Hold out your hand to be read—
you will cross water.
Cup it over your ear.
What calls? What answers?

What calls? What answers?

The moon calls and the salt
answers. The knife calls
and the sun answers.
What did Cain learn,
except that stone calls blood?
Some days the sea is brine and stillness,
the sails limp and the compass spinning.
Then again, the heart is pulled
by every fragment of the earth.

What do we hold to?

This sweet world—how we love it.
As an old horse loves the harness,
loves the stall. The drenching smell
of leather. The work and rest.
The sweat and hay.
Dust-slanted, cricket-singing, the barn—
even when it's burning.

What turns us?

The beauty of the world
is a moon's beauty:
shifting, breathless, mirrored,
a beauty of contradictions. We are tender
because the light is spilling out of October,
a low swoop across the cut
and ragged fields, the bales.
Loneliness rises: a great planet.
Tidal, we cannot turn from it.

What remembers?

Skin. Scars. Stones
from the river. Language like a basket
made for carrying water.
The nest of mice
in the box of papers.

What rises?

The bread, regardless,
in the warm kitchen.
Even if the phone rings,
even if you fold to the floor in grief.
As sparks fly upward, the fever.
And lark song in the evening.

What is asked of us?

More than we can give
and we give it. We bury children
or die bearing them. This is to do
with the size of the brainpan
with respect to the pelvis.
The cost of language
and the root of gentleness:
that we are born helpless.
That we remain, helpless.

What do we hope for?

For hope itself, for honey
at the bottom of bitter tea.
Though hope keeps us pulling loads
that would break the hearts of horses.
In lifeboats we strain our eyes
for a white curl that might be either sail
or wave.

What can heal us?

Landmines cannot return our legs,
but the tumbling world
makes lights of us:
the sea turns glass to milk,
a teacup handle
to a tool for divination.

What can save us?

To be saved is wild and possible.
It is the moth that is born with no mouth.
It is the knife so sharp its edge cannot be seen.
For centuries it was believed
that swallows wintered at the bottom of wells.
Science has seen them
pulled up in buckets, their hearts still beating.

What remains?

The clue's in how we're buried:
dates like time, dog-eared,
a code for breath that's called
our names. What's left is tags
and outlines: words, a score, a scattering
of genes. That's all, unless loss
has substance—that slant of light
that makes us turn and look.

it's late

Curie a Ghost

Seventy years and touch
lingers. With a Geiger counter
you can trace my hand: here it rested,
here. The doorknob clicks and you shiver
as if before the thorny reliquary.
Don't make a saint of me. I touched things.
Men. History will admit I loved three, and forget
that on the battlefield I saw three million.
I pierced them, X-ray. Oh daughters.
I know what it is to go blind and have one's eyes
cut open. I know what it is to walk through walls.
I am more quantum than they let me be, and more
than half alive. I slept with radium
and it entered me. It spun my bones until my breath itself
turned radon. I know I glowed. But I am not a saint
or martyr. Move my bones where you like but I will not stand
for less than everything. They struck my lab and built it again
without the radiation—though they had to lock my notebooks up
in lead. They're slowly blazing.

How to write at the end of the world

Gather what you need.
A pen. A pencil. In a pinch
your fingernails. Paper, but you can write on water
even as it's rising. Write the things you love. Snail shells:
their galaxy spiral, their soft colours softer inside. You too
must build a home from your own body,
light and strong. You too must make your inner self
all feet. Learn to grip and taste
with toes—petal, pebble, road.
Write other shells. Fresh pencil shavings. Beloved
coffee cups and gardens. Spice jars.
Four kinds of salt. A stack
of foxed-up notebooks, that wall of river stones
you set by hand. Write nouns but try
not to list the names. Some stones are too much to move.
Catch gestures: your daughter, just walking, a tug on your fingers,
the arch of your husband's shoulder as he passes up the
     suitcase,
your mother's thumb in the groove of your elbow, her nail
     pressing
a crescent moon. Write down the towns you've left,
colour every wall and rug and cushion. Write down the dog
you named after the moon.
List the kinds of light: the holy dance
of a single candle, the desk lamp
with its brassy shade, the cool light like watered milk
late in the winter. There is a light that loves the bowls of spoons,
a square of sun that swings across the empty floor,

a blue that lives in depths and distance. It's late,
but list the things you love. It's late, but love.
It's late, but has been late always.
The first human things were pressure flakes and notches,
stone knives and reindeer carved from reindeer bones.
It was late, then, in Mal'ta, ice-age Siberia,
when a pendant of a flying swan
was pulled free from a necklace *V* of flying swans
and buried with a child.
The people built their homes of bone there—
took mammoth bones and lived inside them.
The swan may have meant *spring*. It may have meant
to travel. All neck, its wings swept back, its shape
recalls a pen. It may have meant: *keep this*.
It may have meant: *return*. I write because I love this world
and I am losing it. I write because I love this life
and I am losing it. Lost comes from a Nordic word:
los, disband the army. Let go of my hand.
I need to lose my sword. I want to be lost
like a snail on a gravestone, like a deer in the mountains,
with each fern a welcome. Lost like a tossed antler,
like rain falling into water, like a woman in a market
with every spice a home. I want to use my life up
like a pencil. I want to eat stone and leave behind
the shell of a word I live inside,
something open, something with an *o*:
loss/love   long/now   bone/world
home.

A Poet's Citations

Some terms used in texts
Recombination: In physics, "recombination" refers to the epoch in the very young universe when the charged protons and electrons combined into electrically neutral hydrogen, letting light pass through.

History: Mathew Brady is most famous for his battlefield photographs of the Civil War—particularly his exhibit *The Dead of Antietam*.

Skiagraphs
The Curie poems in are deeply indebted to *Radioactive: Marie & Pierre Curie: A Tale of Love and Fallout* by Lauren Redniss (It Books, 2010). This mixed media biography of Curie was an essential source of both detail and emotion. With the exception of the epigraph to "Curie in Love," the quotations from Curie, throughout, come to me through Redniss, who mostly had them from Curie's book *Autobiographical Notes*. Some are elided.

Skiagraphs, 1895: This poem draws from *Naked to the Bone: Medical Imaging in the Twentieth Century*, by Bettyann Holtzmann Kevles (Basic Books, 1998).

The Radium Girls: I met Amelia Maggia (whose name is pronounced a-MAL-ia MAD-ja) in *The Poisoner's Handbook: Murder and the Birth of Forensic Medicine in Jazz Age New York* by Deborah Blum (Penguin, 2011).

What is Eden but a thing that's lost: Among the scientific work done in the Chernobyl Exclusion Zone is a study of disordered spiderwebs by American biologist Timothy Mousseau.

The heart can heal and here is how we know: I learned about this technique for estimating how fast cells turn over—a field called "bomb pulse dating"—from the podcast *Radiolab*.

Beauty/Cost
The Bus Stop: I heard about the bus stop at the German senior care centre from the podcast *Radiolab*.

Ghazals
My dive into ghazals began with Lorna Crozier's book *Bones in Their Wings: Ghazals* and with Crozier's essays, which led me deeper. Ghazals are traditionally a Persian form involving call and response, and my use of borrowed couplets pays tribute to that. I've written many ghazals renga style with my friend Seánan Forbes. Here and there one of the couplets originated from that joint project.

Lorna Crozier: This couplet is from one of the untitled ghazals in *Bones in Their Wings: Ghazals* (Radiant Press, 2003).

Ferenc Juhász: The lines here are actually the title of a famous long poem, "The Boy Changed into a Stag Cries Out at the Gate of Secrets," as translated by Ted Hughes. I came across it in Ted Hughes' collection *Selected Translations* (Farrar, Straus & Giroux, 2007).

Yiannis Ritsos: The lines here are from Ritsos's monologue "Moonlight Sonata," as translated by translated by Peter Green and Beverly Bardsley, in *The Fourth Dimension* (Princeton University Press, 1993).

János Pilinszky: The lines here are from "Van Gogh's Prayer," as translated by George Gömöri, in *Poetry* magazine (Volume 191: 6, 2008).

Theodore Roethke: These lines are the opening of the third section of "The Far Field 1964" from *Collected Poems* (Anchor, 1974).

Wisława Szymborska: These lines are the opening of "The Three Oddest Words," as translated by Clare Cavanagh, from *Poems: New and Collected* (Ecco, 2000).

Anna Akhmatova: These lines are the opening of "You Will Hear Thunder," as translated by DM Thomas, in *Anna Akhmatova: Selected Poems* (Penguin Classics, 1992).

Pablo Neruda: These lines are the close of "Sonnet XVII," as translated by Mark Eisner, from *The Essential Neruda: Selected Poems* (City Lights, 2004).

Acknowledgements

Years and years ago, when there were wolves in Wales, I was a university student studying high energy particle physics. I loved it, for the smart people, for the challenge of the work, and for the joy of knowing the universe more deeply.

I loved the poetry of it: the strange and charm quarks, spin, supersymmetry, asymptotic freedom. Those words melt me. I remember going to one of my mentors, Professor Janet Seger, because I couldn't quite wrap my head around this property quarks have called "colour." Things with colour, like quarks, are affected by the strong nuclear force, the way things with charge are affected by the electromagnetic force. But clearly quarks weren't dipped in buckets of paint. So, I asked, what is colour? "I don't know," my teacher said. "What is charge?"

I thought I knew—but in trying to answer I jerked to a stop. In fact, no one can answer. We think we know "charge" only because we named it—because we've taken Adam's power over it. But we don't really, any more than we understand the interiority of tigers.

We name what we know and we know what we name. But only to a point. The tigerness of tigers will always be a mystery. That was one moment when I understood I didn't need to study physics—I needed to write about it.

Another: I also studied poetry at university, on the side. I completed two honours senior theses—one in physics, of course, and one a chapbook of poems. My mentor for the poems was Professor Brent Spencer. When I graduated, he gave me a copy of *Science and Other Poems* by Alison Hawthorne Deming. I have it still. The title poem came to me as a force of revelation: science is not off-limits as a subject of poetry.

A third: about fifteen years ago, it struck me out of the blue that an equation is metaphor. They both say, *this is that.* Energy *is* matter. The sound of the wind in green wheat = a scythe being sharpened. I told this to the incredible poet Jane Hirshfield, who I am honored to count as a friend. She gave me an eye-brightening smile and said: "Of course." I started writing these poems.

This book has been the work of at least a decade. I have wandered from it off into other poetic projects. I have written whole novels, and published five of them. But here is my book of equations at last.

I want to thank all the people who have stood by me and supported me for that decade. My writing friends on the WELL. My in-person writing group, the Hopeful Writers: Susan Fish, Pamela Mulloy, Kristen Mathies, Nan Forler, and the late Esther Regehr. My dear friend and ghazal partner Seánan Forbes. My friends at my local literary journal, *The New Quarterly*, who were my first door into the literary community in Canada when I immigrated here. I want particularly to thank poetry editor Barb Carter and founding editor Kim Jernigan.

Individual poems from this book have appeared in journals and anthologies, including *Best Canadian Poetry 2018, Best Canadian Poetry 2020, ARC Poetry Magazine, The Fiddlehead, Grain, The Malahat Review, The New Quarterly, Prairie Fire, PRISM international,* and *Rattle.* "How to write at the end of the world" was written for the stage, and performed at *Home Truths,* an International Women's Day event in support of refugees held at the Registry Theatre in Kitchener, Ontario, in March 2020 (at the end of the world, as it happened).

The Ontario Arts Council, particularly through its recommender grants, has been crucial to both making ends meet and keeping my confidence at some minimally functional level throughout the long labour of this book. I must particularly thank *The New Quarterly* and Wolsak and Wynn who have recommended me to this program several times through the decade.

I want to thank my physics mentors, from that lost age: Professors Michael Cherney and Janet Seger. I am now a science writer at Perimeter Institute for Theoretical Physics, and I want to thank that place, and especially fellow science writer, boss, and friend, Natasha Waxman, who lets me hare off after startling, beautiful things.

Finally, I am deeply indebted to the team at Brick Books: In particular, Nick Thran has been a generous and insightful editor, and a patient one. He's strengthened individual poems, and helped me restructure the manuscript. It wouldn't be half the book it is without him.

Erin Noteboom was trained as a particle physicist, and held student jobs at Los Alamos Labs and the CERN supercollider before a health crisis made her reconsider her life and put poetry in the middle of it. This is her third book of poetry, but the first to use the tools and mine the riches of science. Erin has a secret identity as children's novelist Erin Bow—her six novels include the modern classic *Plain Kate* and the Governor General Literary Award-winning *Stand on the Sky*—and a day job as a science writer for the Perimeter Institute for Theoretical Physics. She lives in Kitchener, Ontario.